The Principle of Reciprocity

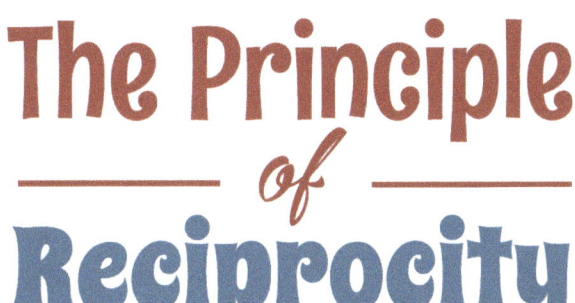

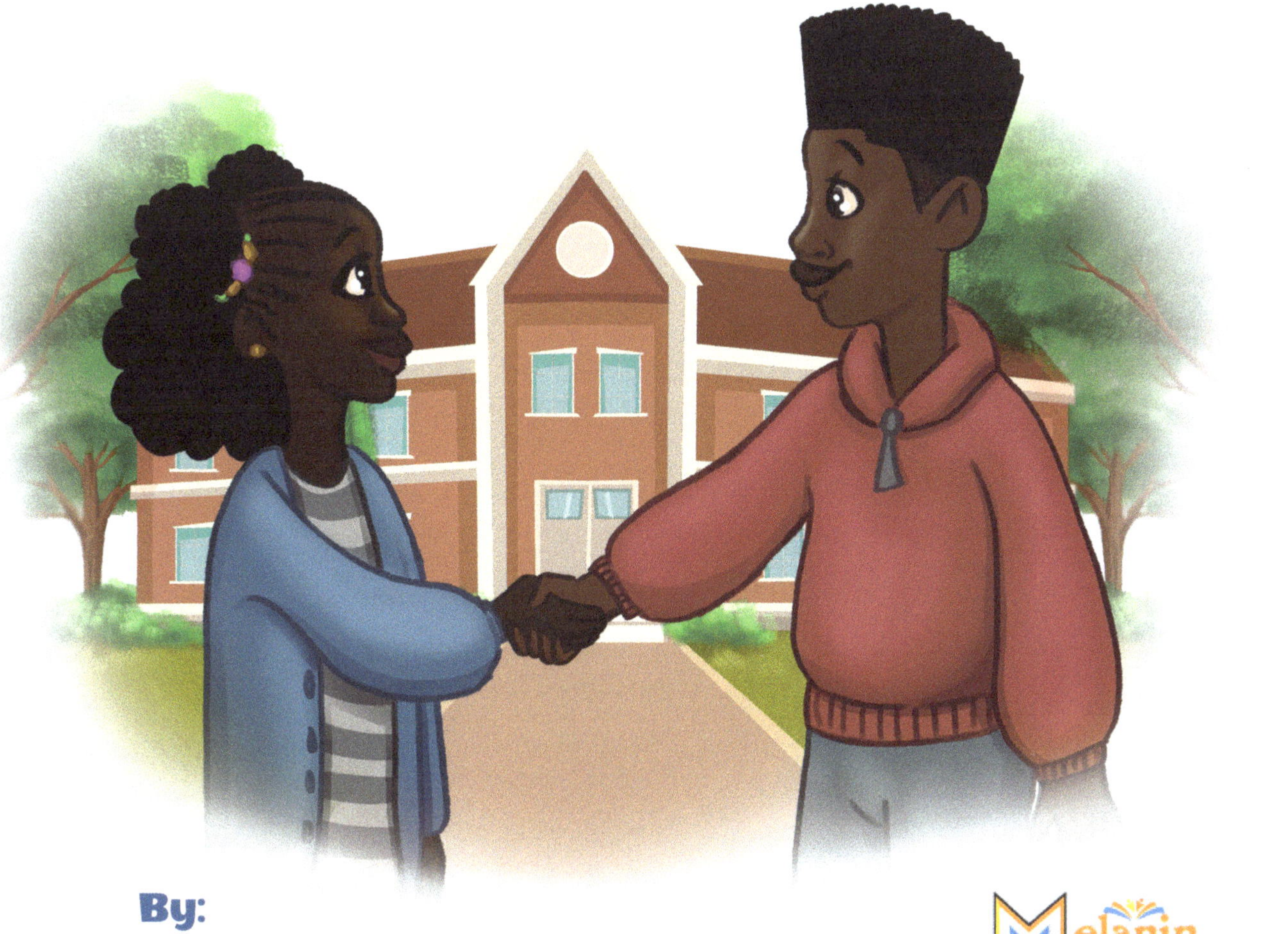

By:
Aimee Lary

Melanin Origins

Published by Melanin Origins

PO Box 122123; Arlington, TX 76012

All rights reserved, including the right of reproduction in whole

or in part in any form.

Copyright 2022

First Edition

The author asserts the moral right under the Copyright, Designs and Patents Act of 1988 to be identified as the author of this work.

This novel is a work of fiction. The names, characters and incidents portrayed in the work, other than those clearly in the public domain, are of the author's imagination and are not to be construed as real. Any resemblance to actual persons, living or dead, events or localities, is entirely coincidental.

All rights reserved. No part of this publication may be reproduced, stored in a retrieval system or transmitted, in any form by any means without the prior consent of the author, nor be otherwise circulated in any form of binding or cover other than that with which it is published and without a similar condition being imposed on the subsequent purchaser.

Library of Congress Control Number: 2021942164

ISBN: 978-1-62676-525-2 hardback

ISBN: 978-1-62676-526-9 paperback

ISBN: 978-1-62676-066-0 ebook

The Principle of Reciprocity

"There is a motion to life; a system of giving and receiving; a rhythm of cause and effect to every aspect of creation. I will do unto others as I would have them do unto me."

www.MelaninOrigins.com

Thankfully, the day started off great! My teacher, Mrs. Scott, is the nicest, and I'm not just saying that because she gave us candy for breakfast. All my classmates were friendly too, well, except for Gabe.

While Mrs. Scott was taking attendance, she called my name – Tommy Young, but Gabe began to laugh and call me "Tommy Old".

He even made fun of Jewel's backpack and called it "baby pack" just because it had unicorns on it.

It was sad to watch him bully my new classmates. His parents must have never told him that whatever you do to others, good or bad, will come back to you.

Some people think they can do anything to anyone and get away with it. They never believe the day will come that they will have to pay for their wrongs, but as for Gabe...

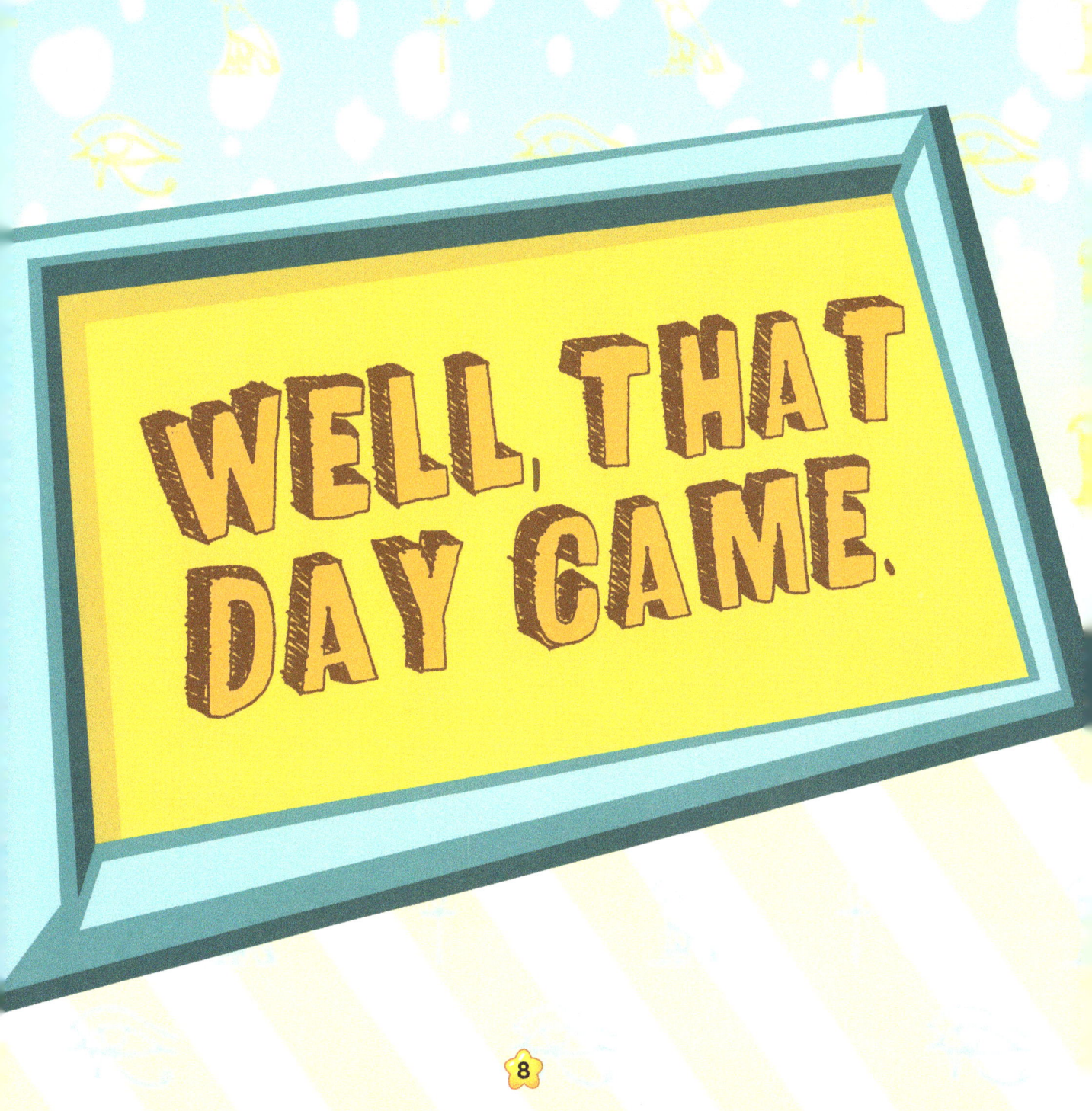

As my sister, Tasha, walked to her seat in the cafeteria, Gabe came from nowhere and pushed her to the ground sending her food tray flying out of her hands.

I was not in the cafeteria at the time, but everyone at school kept talking about a boy being mean to a new kid in the cafeteria.

Yet, just as I was about to score big on the basketball court, I saw Gabe being mean to another student.

She stood between the two of us and reminded me what our parents taught us: whatever you do to others, good or bad, will come back to you.

I wanted payback for my sister, but suddenly, the feeling of anger and frustration went away and the spirit of forgiveness came over me.

The crowd disappeared and only Gabe and Tasha remained. With great appreciation, Gabe apologized and thanked Tasha for helping him when she did not have to. In return, he made a promise to always treat her and others with kindness and respect.

Modern Day Melanin Origins

This book is dedicated to the well-beloved scholar of scholars Kaba Kamene.

Professor Kaba Hiawatha Kamene is the bestselling author of *Spirituality Before Religions* and *Honoring Professor William Leo Hansberry (1894-1965): An Intellectual Libation For The Architect Of America's African Studies Department*. He is recognized as an internationally acclaimed, Pan African Historian.

Originally born as Booker Taliaferro Coleman Jr. in New York City, Professor Kamene became an esteemed Educator, Consultant, Curriculum and Community Developer, and most recently is the Principal Facilitator and Chief Executive Officer of an African Centered Science Academy named, "Per Ankh (Temple/House Of Life)." Kaba believes that culture plays a vitally important role in education and proudly credits many of his academic views to his teacher, world-renowned educator, Dr. John Henrik Clarke.

~ UnitedBlackLibrary.org

www.ingramcontent.com/pod-product-compliance
Lightning Source LLC
Chambersburg PA
CBHW040013080526
44586CB00028B/2996